SOLSTICE

SOLSTICE

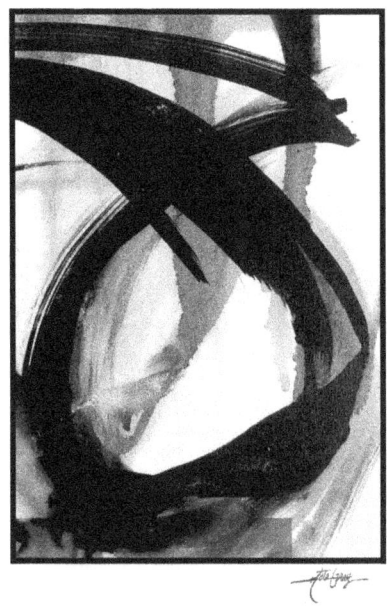

Kathleen Cain

© Kathleen Cain 2022

All rights reserved. No part of this book may be reproduced or transmitted in any form or by any means, electronic or mechanical or by any information or storage and retrieval system without permission in writing from the author or publisher.

Cover art and section break illustrations © Kate Gray
All rights reserved. Used with permission.

Layout and design by Yolanda Ciolli

Published by Compass Flower Press
Columbia, Missouri

ISBN 978-1-951960-40-7

My introduction to magic came early when my sister and I were given the book *Fanta Sea Children* by Vere L. Mathews, and eventually led me to the magical world of poetry.

Table of Contents

Sleeping Alone

Wanderers 1
Dimensions 2
Mud 3
The Visitor 4
Mosaic 5
Guaranteed 6
Parchment 7
Karst 8
Orchids 9
No Cast Shadow 10
Tree Rings 11
Mobius 12
Last Dance 13

Night Vision

Moon Shadow 17
Super Moon 18
Shadow of Evening 19
Wind 20
Tornado Season 21
The Cardinal 22
Bee's Wing 23
From Ovid 24
Awakening 25
Tiny Poet 26
Touching Memory 27
Milkweed Messages 29
Maple Syrup Sorrow 30
Ashes 31

Shapeshifters

Looking for Light 35
Walrus 36
Androids 37
When? 38
How Dare You 39
Shame 41
Better Instincts 42

At the Ready 43
Being White 44
Mother's Day 45

Uninvited

Ida 49
The Shadow 50
Weariness 51
The Nest 52
Assault 53
Rage 54
Broken Wings 55
A Son's Tale 56
The Virus 57
Dignity 58
In a Rowboat with Obama 59

Nostalgia

Of Memory 63
Bulletins to the Family 64
Birdsong 62
Oil and Salt 66
Vega's Fairies 67
A Different Turn 68
Clear Water 69
Aspen 70
The Lake 71
Pyrenees 72

Rapt

Violin 77
Elegant Strings 78
Woodland Symphony 79
The Cool 80
Orchid Opus 81
Bonnie's Palette 82
Cold 83
Guitar and Voice 84
Cold Morning 85
Otherworld Orchestra 86
Equinox 87

Sleeping Alone

Wanderers

Where will my memories go when I leave?
Perhaps they will search for places to land
As those I love dream.

Perhaps they might mingle with strangers

Or become wanderers
Awaiting the sighting of a port
In which they can navigate a landing.

This New Year's Eve I am sending a cache out
To find a new home

As I rest.

Dimensions

I think I'm knocking on another dimension
Just beyond the one in which I dwell.
Travelers to Mars may witness its timelessness
As remnants of life are discovered.

Time
So restrictive
Closes our borders and controls our thoughts

To what end I wonder.

I chase each thought
As though its speed were earthly.

Sleep often offers images,
Clues

To what I cannot know
Yet feel deeply.

Mud

I don't exist in this happy world
Although I do indulge
As if content.

Joy, yes
Passion, yes.

Yet
Blood has appeared
Crimson hints at first

A red hue in running water
Pale enough to ignore

Prescient for what's next
As our flesh
Runs together

Moving as a river
To tomorrow.

The Visitor

I noticed a subtle cooling
As though evening had come early
Knowledge that he had arrived.

Familiar,
Yet unseen.

I felt his arms as they wrapped around my waist
His form drew me close,
An embrace, of sorts.

Softly, he spoke to my back,
"It's time."

Then, "You'll feel a slight tug."

I thought of a carrot, being released from loamy soil.

Mosaic

Light and shadow play
Competing for my delight

They ask me to leave the darkness
Shed worry
Welcome hope

The shape and color of leaves
Form patterns
Into a growing mosaic

Fall's treat
A gallery
On which I stroll

I struggle to stay in this time
As though it may be my last

As winter descends
And gentle snow covers all.

Guaranteed

As though entering a cave
Embarking on this journey
Where lighting is poor
And weariness lingers

A place where the road is unmapped
Risk guaranteed

Yet compelling me forward
Is an energy stored deep
To be called on if asked

Knowing this place for years
Yet seeing it is a sorrowful surprise

It is clear as spring water
Storing all that is needed

And so, go

Many have gone before
And many will follow.

Parchment

Fragile parchment, aged by time
Guards my knowledge
      of what's beyond

So that I can see only bits
Tiny pieces beyond this curtain
Their fullness blocked.
By gravity, time, life itself

And yet, I know.

Karst

That place we know
Not by name

There below the path I walk

It is where streams disappear
My body feels the faint echo that tells me

Where I will go

Limestone and water merge and make that which resonates
Cavernous places prepared for me

In time I will reside there.

Orchids

In deep winter
Snow and ice collect in grim reality
On the roof below
As I sit with my orchids

I breathe
Take in the beauty
Wonder at the rhythm
Of life and cold

Its unrelenting trueness
As I proceed
A road whose end is unknown

GPS useless
Prayer a joke

Only the in and out of breath exists.

No Cast Shadow

I go through periods of emptiness
As though on a sunny day I cast no shadow

Today, I visited an aging couple just moved to a care facility
And remember the riotous fun
When they owned the magical house on a creek

There, we gathered watercress
Or wandered naked after a wine filled dinner
And slept with smiles.

It is evening
And days before a winter full moon.

Its rays will fill my bedroom.

Tree Rings

The sunset is on time
Its ETA certain.

Tree rings remind me of my mortality
My eyes move from the recent outer layer
To the center
Its oldest core
Perhaps a sapling
A time before me.

As I move through my own passage
I glimpse the real nature of being
Stripped from the costume of identity.

I am here and I am alone
Moving to a conclusion
Preordained in the womb.

Mobius

I cannot comprehend
Even though I feel
The mystery

A journey that never seems to end

No matter how hard I try
I do not see the horizon
Of this period

The feel of the infinite
So elusive

Now inside me
As I start each day

That which I cannot envision

My very being is on this new plane.

Last Dance

Sorrow's ribbon weaves through me
A snake-like rhythm
I look for light
As he tightens around me

I dance
Hips releasing the fear
Its inevitable closeness

Come
Dance with me
One last time.

Night Vision

Moon Shadow

I saw her light on the floor beside my bed
Its brightness casting magic
Across the room.

Later, I rose and looked out the window

She was high in the sky
Dressed in organza, ready for the Prom.

She did not speak to me
Instead, she retreated behind her veil of clouds.

Coy
Soon, she will be full.

Super Moon

A soft breeze is a gift
After this winter of plague

Pleasure envelopes me as I open my eyes
To see the sky, visible through budding trees

The evensong of birds ushers in the night

 Invites me to sleep

A nourishing super moon, just starting to wane
Will visit me towards dawn
Sated, I will return to visions in darkness

And then morning
And gentle springtime.

Shadow of Evening

I note a cardinal perched on a bare branch
Just outside my window
Colors vanished in the shadow of early evening

Perhaps a proud male
But what do I know
As colors are muted

Just that life goes on
I await full dark

Followed with the surprise of another morning
When the cardinal's color will be revealed

Vivid red of the male
Or dusty female.

Either way
Spring is here for some.

Wind

A low moan
Barely discernable
Brings on this evening

I wonder where it had been
Before it crossed into my space

Is it here to tell me?
Something I need to know
Something I'm ignoring
In this closed-in space?

Newly leaved trees
Reflect all kinds of light

So much more than winter

Branches nudge one another
Whisper their secrets

Fold them in for the coming night
To be released into my dreams

Help me to understand
What I cannot hear.

Tornado Season

Wind, that unseen force
Moves leafless trees
Sight and sound telling me of its strength

Sun drifts into the room where I sit
A welcome treat
Its nourishing light toying with me

Seducing my solitude
Asking me to play

Shadow fingers join the mix
Prelude to dark and the end to this day

Soon, daffodils will finish their joyous display

Leaves, buds, and storms will follow.

The Cardinal

I watched her transport the twigs
Now a nest
Just outside my window.

She settles in
Her head a periscope
Searching for intruders
Following her DNA

Her dull brown color is a perfect camouflage
Only her reddish beak and bandit eyes stand out
Warnings.

Something disturbs her and she flies to a nearby tree
I can hear the clicks from the bright red male
As he guards the nest, now unprotected

Minutes pass
She returns
Settles
And peace ensues

Belying the dangers ahead.

Bee's Wing

Her skin was translucent
Rare and fine

She ran wild
Moving on spring's breezes
Till she found a place safe and warm

Shielded from the wind and sun
Where she could grow

Beauty comes from a place
Such as this.

(Thanks to Richard Thompson)

From Ovid

A field that has rested gives a beautiful crop.
—Ovid

Should I lie in that field for a night, or more —
I might hear the movement of insects, the call of an owl,
Perhaps see the moon peek out from clouds passing through.

I would be with evening as it led to a night whose embrace
    would lull me
To let go, indulge in matters of nature that have little to do with
    my days.

I long for this time of light, shadow then dark.
A place to contemplate my species
Find peace with creatures that know with certainty where they
    belong.
Stay with wonder.

A bird closes its wings for sleep
A cat curls under a porch
A dog signals with its paw to be let in.

Soon sleep will come in this lush place
Where all that matters is the stillness of being and belonging.

When I awake, stretch and stand
I will be refreshed.

Damp with dew I'll walk in the days ahead
Filled with gratitude in the knowing.

Awakening

It is spring. Packed deep in the ground, plants are seeking their way up, feeling the softness of warm rain. Hostas curl, slyly masquerading their mighty size into cones as they burrow up. Wildflowers, too numerous to name announce their dominance of the early green, offer pleasure to those of us who walk.

Within me, another spring has announced itself, memories that need the cool clean air of now, parts that may bring shame, sadness or simply something other that I need to understand. Perhaps it is my draw to darkness….

I'm still coiled, yet ready to seek the warmth above ground, the part I know is the me I cannot connect to others, the alien me who wonders of my origin.

I wait, seeking perhaps.

Tonight, it is cool, so I can rest, await the pull of heat when it finds me and beckons me up and out where I will see and be seen.

Tiny Poet

She peeks over the horizon
Searches the landscape for safety
A rising sun lights up the new growth

She spreads her wings
To see if she can still fly
After hiding in shadows these four years.

A gentle breeze softly lifts her
Until her body rises
And she moves

I feel her shadow pass
Her watchful presence
So welcome

My tears join others as we ascend
From our hiding places.

A tiny poet
Invites us to follow her

Hands joined.

Touching Memory

A reflection in a pond
Built by trees and sun
Or a cloud formation building before a storm
A shadow, perhaps
Even a dream

They without my bidding
Each has something to say
Wordless, they show themselves
Then dissolve
Leaving their memory

Now, imprinted on my brain
Part of the vast storage
Which, sometimes at my bidding
Returns
Carrying messages

Then, just before the words appear
The clarity I so desire
They vanish
To rest, just below my consciousness

I grasp at these faces, these beings without flesh
That other world I know exists
The one that surrounds me
Teases me
Melts
Just in time

Sometimes I see those I've lost to this region
They surround me as a cloak
That gives off no warmth

I try to grasp it
Hold it up to the light
As it dissolves from my touch
Recedes
Waits
Returning only when I forget.

Milkweed Messages

Crisp winter shadows on new snow
Adorn my morning walk.

A stand of milkweed pods emptied of seed
marks a field edged by barren trees

Tiny messengers long gone on fall breezes
The remaining menacing shapes remind me of crocodile heads

I think of them as dark approaches on this winter night
Wraithlike figures pass across the snow.

I follow their silent movement
Soundless, prescient

Perhaps they contain the messages of the milkweed.

Maple Syrup Sorrow

It takes just the right conditions to run.

One day nothing
Then another tap and out it comes
Golden and clear
Filling the vessel you've been holding.

As it flows you can only watch

Knowing it will end one day

Later to be reduced to a dark liquid
to be stored.

Cherished, it will be consumed with love
When you need it most.

Ashes

We are reduced to this
A soft pile
From what was once
A flame

A few embers remain
So I blow
Watch the red glow deep within

I add paper
Search for dry twigs
And lay them with care across the tiny spark
I ask for help

A weak figure dances in the breeze
We add more wood
It catches

Hope flares
It will take time and care

Slowly we tend to the blaze
Lest it vanish again.

Shapeshifters

Looking for Light

The crack that lets it in is just beyond the horizon
It beckons to me
As though I know how to fly

I did once
Young enough to see joy
To soar and land
And sleep the sleep of dreams

I would later learn of war, disease
The flaws of our species

I long to muster the energy to pull that wonder in
Store it till I'm full

And then, share it.

Walrus

Science be damned
He lumbers
Toward the helicopter

Reporters shout out
Under the blades' din

This spectacle
Arose from the collected will
Of many
Who thought they were victims

Sped on by the fire breath of this dragon

This creature fueled by greed
Lured those who will ultimately be hurt

One day his gluttony will reach its pinnacle

Sated, he will abandon those victims who raised him high
They will vanish in a landslide with no exit.

Androids

Each new day without the viper
Gives my body more rest
Winter's sunshine,
Food for my withered soul

I shudder at memories of the invasion
Not long ago

Men with hate in their eyes
Moved as androids under his command

Vampires
Intent on draining goodness

The malevolent clan watched the televised spectacle
As though entertainment

People died
As it was warned in Georgia
Where red bled into purple
Perhaps saving the nation.

When?

My tears have been lurking for days
Just behind my eyes
As I pass through one news day to another.

The destruction of joy
My faith in country
The loss of connection
As power reigns
Blind to the citizens who make up our nation.

I hear one after another excuse
For the behavior of the behemoth

A bull run loose
While those who could help
Shrink behind the veil
Robbing the people of their voice.

My verse
Often of wonder with all that is joy
Has dried

Cold tree limbs
Against a pale winter sky.

Will this end?

How Dare You

Walk into my sacred rooms
Plant your butts in my polished chairs
Saunter on my marble floors
Take my money

And look the other way

How dare you
Ignore my pain
Watch those who sent you
Suffer and die

How dare you
Turn your obsequious faces to the clown
Who pulls your strings
As you succumb to his demands

Bow your heads
Walk in his lazy shoes
Do his bidding

How dare you
Praise his buffoonery

How dare you tolerate his entitled children
Who, appointed to advise him
Are paid with my money
As they enrich themselves

They appear as royalty
Answer to no one

People die as he tweets and drives his little red golf cart

The big plane
Sacred once

Has become a shuttle to his resorts
Where the chosen pay to curry favor.

People die as pillaging drains our country.

How Dare You

I will sleep tonight
Allow hope to seep into my veins
Those vessels dried by sorrow welcome the coming rain

How dare you come near me.

Shame

Tears pool as I watch the news
So many shamed by need

Rounded shoulders, eyes downcast
People move forward
Ready to receive

This Indignity is new to most.

Others, in cars
Move in infinite snaking lines

These cars are the kind seen parked at malls
On ordinary weekends
Families out shopping

Now, windows are rolled down as masked volunteers approach
Place sacks inside,
back up and wave them on

Inside, parents scan the covered faces
Find the eyes
Look for pity and seeing none, breathe out

They drive on
Making room for the next car.

And so it goes
The radio reports a story
About a basketball team of millionaires
When caught, paying back the loan from this government

At least there will be supper tonight.

Better Instincts

I like where I go these early cold nights
Especially when meals taste good
A bath is warm.

COVID still roams, but our doors are closed
And worries slim.

I like where I go these days since the vote
The surge from all
To call on better instincts.

The venom of losing is dissipating
Yet still the rattlesnake
Raises its head above its coil
Looking for prey.

This will take time.

But I like where I go these nights
As the days lengthen

My heart is full with all that has passed
I sit and let cold knowing seep in
So I never forget what happens
When we look the other way.

At the Ready

I have slowed from a waltz to a drift
As though my mind and body no longer care
Direction is minimal and has little value.

Masks are being lazily dropped
First off one ear
Then forgotten when we wander into stores.

I see but do not hear
I look without interest
I care but cannot locate passion

All that energy
Spent managing fear
Is dissolving
Relocating in a sphere I do not yet see

And so
I read
I walk
I indulge in not knowing
As fear retreats to its own place

Always at the ready.

Being White

I am a voyeur filled with envy

For the dignity, courage, and strength it takes
To be black in this white world.

To navigate a life in this sea
Roiling with power
To keep people down.

And yet they rise
Move in the delicious flow of Black and Brown wonder
Beauty unmatched.

I want to join.
But perhaps my initiation starts with notice
To not look away from the struggle.

Mother's Day

This has been a lovely day
Clear cool air with soft winds
Leaves sprinkle the light
Playing with shadows
Inviting me to join the frolic

Meanwhile grief wraps its arms around me
Holds me still
Gentle, yet certain I have something to learn.

News forces me to open
Take in as much as I can bear
Not leave the sorrow to others.

However it takes form
I must own the awfulness of my species

Take back my own raggedy bits.

Uninvited

Ida

The winds join forces
Over warm water
Mapping an assault

Soulless storm
Born of a humanity
Fueled by greed

Its eye is probing with calm purpose.

We name them
As though in doing so
We can bargain for our folly

As the orb scans the horizon
And plans its approach

Mortals scatter.

The Shadow

It emerged unseen this spring
Crossed oceans, fields, towns, and bodies
Submerging itself into our very breath

The Greeks say it is born of chaos

When the sun shines
We think we see it

As we sleep it comes to us

Its release is uncertain
Its travels unannounced

As we move it follows
Looking for a door.

Weariness

It flows into pores
Takes over days
As we move forward
Dodging a virus
While witnessing the horror
Of ourselves

Predators
Of those who lack privilege
By their birth

I attempt to own
And express kindness

As I take in air
May I exhale into a kinder universe.

The Nest

It happened as news grew better
Things were opening up

I could feel my chest filling with reluctance

Going out
Joining in
After so long laced in fear

Deeper within
A new companion spoke

He moved swiftly to embrace me

Gently sinister, he spoke
"You're mine now."

I sank into the dark nest he'd made for me this spring.

Assault

I noticed her as she approached the exit
Young, attractive, her hair bound up in a bandanna
She was eating and walking
Some kind of take out in a bowl.

I was leaving the store
After practicing social distance.

She burst into the exit I had just entered
Brushed past me as she continued to eat

She was close enough to touch me.

It felt like an assault
What did it matter to her?

She is young enough to survive this virus.

I felt I had to return to the store and did.
At a safe distance I told her of my fear and offense.

As I spoke, she tried to suppress a grin but failed.

To her I was the seventy-five year old white woman
A class of people for whom she may have had plenty of reason to
  feel contempt.

I felt invisible for who I really am
And left gathering up my fury and hurt

And wondering what had been done to her in her short life.

Rage

The burst of rage
So unexpected from a young stranger

You spoke softly to him
About his child
A friendly comment
About the food containers he was sneezing on
Perhaps he could move

Infection
Public health
Spraying saliva across drink boxes
Anyone would want to know

It takes a village
You thought

But you are an old woman
And his look told you
How little you matter in his world

The chasm rising
Between this man
A stranger

And people like you
The ones aging into irrelevance.

Broken Wings

I feel grief
Not quite tears
Just a tightness in my throat

I seek a metaphor
To allow its release

So I can breathe
Appreciate the air
Enjoy food this day

Once I name it
I can put it on a page

Let it emerge from my body

Seen and named
I can keep it from growing inside
As it did
So long ago

I drew that one
A bird with a broken wing

This one is clever
Perhaps because it is so ubiquitous

As though we knew for years
It would ccome
During a time when it would thrive.

A Son's Tale

The New Yorker, April 13, 2020

As I read the story I was eating ramen
An idle habit
Until my throat closed

It was an account from a son about his father's Corona virus.

Elmhurst Hospital is overwhelmed
No visitors are allowed

In the days after his admission texts between father and son grew fainter

He accounts unanswered calls to doctors
Too busy to even talk

The last text from the father read
"I'm going to sleep. I love you."
The son kept calling
But got no information
Only that the doctors were in a very difficult time
Treating thirty-five critical patients.

Finally a call
His father had passed away

I stared at my food
Then out the window
Took in the lovely green of early spring.

The son is now speculating how and when to plan a funeral.

The feel of ramen remains in my throat.

The Virus

So I am sad, you say
Gossamer feelings pass through my mind

Leaving paths
Arachnid web residue
I cannot see or feel

We descend into isolation

This tiny creature
Culls us

First, from one another
Then, from the mass that is humanity
Only filaments remain

Meanwhile, spiders will weave their webs.

Dignity

This first day of November
The sky is filled with gray clouds that part with the wind
To reveal a brilliant sun
Pouring through falling leaves
Making patterns
Of red, yellow, and green

My dogs and I
Move business-like up the trail and into the woods
The younger one sets a pace we dutifully follow

Further along, the older dog pauses
As though to look at something, or perhaps to sniff
Dropping back as she does

I'm onto her game

The break of stride
As she regains breath and energy
Trotting behind me, slower now
As the lead dog continues
Stopping now and then to see if we are still coming

It is the same technique my mother used
When she ventured out of her apartment
leaving her oxygen tank at home.

In a Rowboat with Obama

I watch, mesmerized as his fine hands stir the still water.

Ripples move outward
Creating a pattern
Infinite.

That lopsided grin adds to the wonder.

If I could take him home, I would

Keep him safe
For another time

When we would deserve him.

Nostalgia

Of Memory

Joy, a droplet of dew
Catches the morning light

Meanwhile clouds gather
Too massive to consider….

In another place
Mountain streams fill with snowmelt
Carrying sunlight down as they tumble along rocks

I follow with my eyes to join the wonder

Ignore the chaos of the darkness that chases the day away

And breathe in the memory.

Bulletins to the Family

Thought, a slow river without rapids
Preceded what he decided to share

His typewriter was his voice
As he sent pieces to us

"Bulletins to the Family"
They arrived in the mail

I still have a few

They bound us from Utah to Kansas to all places where we lived.

Our grandfather, the western Judge
Our patriarch

He is still present in my later days.

Birdsong

It was not quite dark

As we sat together on a bench

A bird sound interrupted our silence

She said, "Robin."

"No Mother, that's not a robin."

"Evensong," she replied.

I miss her to this day.

Oil and Salt

Anchovies were my favorite part of the parties my parents had. We would wait on the stairs until the last guests left. The final couple would usually be Cass and Mary Lou. We all knew that Cass had a crush on Mother but he was my father's best friend. Mary Lou looked like a Mary Lou. She had Botox-like lips. Cass was loud. He and my father were both engineers at McNally Pittsburg. I wanted to grow up to look like Mary Lou, but not to be married to Cass. His wind gusts of talk would mow down all in his path. I did love him, though. I guess I knew that he was our father's friend, and that counted for a lot. Cass seemed to like us better than his own children, whom he often called those, "Goddammed Kids!"

There would always be anchovies left over, their salty little bodies curled into snail like submission, each pierced by a single toothpick, ready for placement on a cracker. I could hardly wait.

After goodbyes silence descended. We kids would rush to the anchovies, snap them into our mouths and when our gustatory event was over, run our fingers over the plate to get up all the oil. We must have needed the salt. Mother always took out half the salt in any recipes since she knew just as Grandmother Woolley did, that salt, sugar, and fat were the killers in family diets.

Anchovies restored the salt and fat simply, quickly and efficiently. Sugar was really hard to locate in our household. After a lifetime of eating well, the damn broke when Mother came to live in our town. I would take her to the grocery store, do my own shopping, and could depend on finding her, leaning over her cane, her face with a beatific smile, in the bakery. She watched the stickiest, most gooey pastries as though they were alive, a good television show perhaps.

Vega's Fairies

Her arrival was meteoric, as though spun from the star for which she is named. The cold January sky sent her down, into a warm infant's bed, complete with residual respiratory sounds from the journey.

Often, I think my mother had to die for her to come, and now she looks down from that same star, visiting from time to time.

When she sleeps she is magical. The fairies she and I know about sit on the bed and watch over her. "Grandmother," she whispers just before she assumes her sleeping position, "are the fairies coming tonight?"

My conspiratorial whisper, "Yes," follows. She closes her piercing eyes and I begin. I place two fingers lightly on her head and move them up and down. "I think they've sent ambassadors down," I say. "They are planning a party."

She keeps her eyes shut tightly as more of my fingers arrive and dance lightly on her head and back. Eyes still shut she pulls her nightshirt up to expose her back to the fairies.

One visit, she brought me a tooth, showing me the bloody spot in her mouth. She'd been working on it all day. That night, when I hoped she was fast asleep, I placed an envelope under her pillow, took the tooth she'd placed there and crept out of the room.

That afternoon a note arrived on my bed. "Grandmother. I know you are the tuth fary." was printed in the hand of a six year old. I herd you."

I put the note in my pocket and said nothing.

That night, at bedtime "Grandmother, are the fairies coming?" Eyes tightly shut she pulled up her nightshirt and our ritual started again.

The night star glowed high in the cold sky.

A Different Turn

It is May and I see caps and gowns
A breeze captures a flowing robe
Exposing high heel shoes
They make her gait awkward

The procession moves toward an auditorium
Gusty breezes accompany the movement of people
Hands keep the tasseled hats in place

Proud relatives move along to sit in the audience
Subdued by a speech as they wait for the flow of graduates

A row at a time rises and proceeds to the stage
Families and friends rise to cheer
Popping up like river otters.

You proceed past this
Think of her.

She took a different turn….

Clear Water

My dogs race through a cut leading to the creek.

They move in unison down the sandy side
And sink soundlessly into the deepest part
Cooling their bellies.

The water, usually still and brown,
Flows clear this warm spring day.

Content, they drink,
Stealing glances up at me
Awaiting my signal to resume our walk.

Aspen

Mountain breezes come with mystery
A shift in light
Perhaps the collision of sun and shade
The sound the same

A haunting presence
Movement passing me by
As I proceed down a familiar trail

An invisible escort
Reminding me of all I do not know

Later
Waves of shadow
Blend the aspen and pine
Rippling across my vision.

A low moan follows
Letting me know evening is coming

When I will settle
Within this magical place.

All is suddenly still
Sunlight washing across the dark of pine and the vibrant Aspen leaves.

The Lake

As I write, my favorite lake is eight hundred miles away and nine thousand, five hundred feet up. Here at sea level I hold this place dear. I know two of its seasons well.

One is full of deep snow, the lake frozen with welcoming footprints inviting a crossing. The other, summer, the lake is swollen with melt and rainfall.

Both offer a silence, deeper than any I know. Moose are around, their stillness foreboding, as encounters are a reminder that I am an intruder to this magical place, expendable if need be.

It is May. This next month the blue columbine will explode in a meadow off the path awakened as the melt feeds the rivers below.

Their delicate shapes defy the harshness of deep winter and invite the delusion that it is a safe place. Beauty and danger go together in this dance, a twirl that intoxicates, makes breath flirt with existence, not taken for granted.

I often imagine nighttime on the lake's edge. The reflection of the moon—washing secrets across its water and sounds I'll never hear.

Large creatures gather in reeds at the lake's edge, their enormous weight creating beds I will see on a morning hike as they proceed down the mountain to their daytime wanders to graze.

Winter will come again, the first sights early at this altitude. Skunk cabbage is often the first to signal change. Snow will soon mute the pines, load branches, followed by soft drifts as cold settles, ominous for those who doubt the ferocity of what is to come.

Pyrenees

My horse stepped lightly
As though his hoofs might interfere with the history we trod

Dust, remnants of buildings
Small huts
From times we cannot recall

When they lived on the ground
Cooked outside

Worshiped gods we do not know

These French mountains
Are cut with deep swaths
Of rivers which drain impossible steepness

The horses know
And are hired to keep us safe

Perhaps from the terrain
But not from what we might know

If we pay attention.

Rapt

Violin

I long for my bow

The connection from string to arm to chin
Most of all the memory of the vibrations in my chest.

This instrument

I wonder
If it was a conduit to the heart
Before Babel

When we knew more
Said less
As a species

I recall these wordless messages with gratitude.

Elegant Strings

The smell of oil combined
With sunlight
Infused a studio
So long ago

Within,
The artist laid down his brush
Silent, he motioned to the model
Done.

Months later
A portrait was hung
The model preserved in colors carefully applied.

The painting hangs there still.

The model grew old
Walked with a cane
Her upper back C shaped.

While the painting continues to host visitors
To view the lasting beauty.

A cello sonata moves as a river
Through galleries
Of loveliness.

Woodland Symphony

Early afternoon stillness
Creeps in

Breezes stop
As clouds gather and fill
Birds grow quiet

As though night is arriving early

We are gathering for a concert
Lights flash signaling a return to our seats.

The conductor steps out
Baton high

An oboe sounds a long A
A rumble of thunder follows.

The Cool

I await its coming

Meanwhile stillness surrounds me

Breathing, an effort
Expending too much energy

Descending each August
The smoldering embrace of heat's cruel arms

I keep quiet
As though I might not be noticed

I sneak a breath
And I'm caught
I will wait longer for the next one.

Orchid Opus

The orchid leaf bends
As though to a conductor
Of music I long to hear

I am infused with the wonder
Of the obedience of this green leaf
A stark canal in its center
To convey water to its roots

Coaxing the reluctant stalk
Which will become a bloom

The plant is inside.
It is October.
I am seduced and will wait.

Bonnie's Palette

Colors
At first subtle

Soft umber
Black
Purple, perhaps

Exploding into
Vivid reds, yellows and blues
Under her hands

The piano drifts with hues that swirl
Blending with dark walls

The coming night

And the souls around her.

Cold

It blew in last night riding on grey November clouds
Moved through the trees
Unburdening them of their now dried leaves

I hear them scurrying along roof tops and sidewalks
As a peacefulness settles in me

I prepare to let go and rest
In winter's embrace.

Guitar and Voice

Upon listening to the guitar and his voice
I am taken to a place I need to go
Away from this day

Away from the loss of humanity
And back to a sense of my own body

As though I can swallow his intonation
Feel the vibrations as they seek my soul
My chest gives way to the strings

I breathe in
Store the pulsations which convey wonder

I see ribbons of sound
Sent to comfort me in this time

Gratefully, I consume and store what I need.

Cold Morning

Stillness greets this winter morning

Formless in face mask, heavy jacket, and mittens
walking on frozen mud

A cloudless sky offers undeterred sun
Together with cold, they create a painting
Of trees, their branches, and me

Silhouettes offer a pageantry as a god might
view the woods before the modesty of leaves
And ourselves stretched across the frozen ground.

Otherworld Orchestra

As her small boat crested the wave, she saw the island
Descending into the trough
Her mind turned to the rhythms of the seas

The conductor's arms wide, inviting
Enticed the soft oboes
Followed by the deep bassoon

Without notice the choir joined, somber
The woodwinds having set the mood.

She allowed the vessel to take her to the shore

Where she would be wrapped in a shroud
Set on the muted waves
Moving into peace in another realm.

Equinox

Sleep, curled against the cold as
Snow, a cloak of soft perfect flakes

Breath slows. Dreams swirl and dance

Enter the deep descent
To a soundless place
They return to the trees as fairies

All thought has now vanished and there you remain till
One day, a slight movement disturbs your rest

Not quite awake
You stretch
Peer out and see
A lengthening shadow

Adjust your position
Monitor the change
And each day forward
The shadow elongates

Until the snow has gone

Growth stirs beneath you

Soon you will fully wake
Stand

Songs of spring greet you

And you stroll
Into the light.

www.ingramcontent.com/pod-product-compliance
Lightning Source LLC
Chambersburg PA
CBHW020212090426
42734CB00008B/1038